JAZLYN
AND THE WHAT IFS

What if... it all worked out? Try to envision the positive!
Renná Bruce

Written by **Renná Bruce**
Illustrations by **Janet Shultis**
Illustration colouring and page design by **Kevin Strang**

Published in Canada by

Jazlyn J & Company Inc.

www.jazlynj.com

Library and Archives Canada Cataloguing in Publication

Title: Jazlyn J & the what ifs / written by Renná Bruce ; illustrated by Janet Shultis.
Other titles: Jazlyn J and the what ifs
Names: Bruce, Renná, 1969- author. | Shultis, Janet, 1962- illustrator.
Description: Series statement: Jazlyn J series
Identifiers: Canadiana 20190122374 | ISBN 9780978180997 (softcover)
Classification: LCC PS8553.R818 J39 2019 | DDC jC813/.6—dc23

This book is dedicated to Beth, Sara and Nicole. Beth, for smiling through the journey and sharing her caring heart. Sara, for always knowing the right thing to say, and in doing so, making those around her feel special and needed in the world. Nicole, for her love of life and love for those who are lucky enough to be in hers. I raise a bean bag to you all.

Renná

This book is dedicated to my siblings Kathy Semple Chow, David Semple and Glen Semple. Your love, support, friendship and respect have lifted me up throughout my life. Our shared stories and memories ground me. Your dedication to your families makes me proud. I cherish the time we spend together. I love you dearly.

Janet

Jazlyn J and her family went to her room to share their favourite parts of the day. Normally, it was Jazlyn's favourite part of the day but tonight, bedtime was different. Very different.

Tomorrow, Jazlyn was going to stand up in front of her entire school and sing a song to honour Mrs. Beggs, who was retiring at the end of the school year. Jazlyn had practiced and practiced. The song was going to be a special tribute. But still, Jazlyn was nervous.

They all shared their favourite parts of the day. Her baby brother Jordie simply nodded and hugged Jazlyn. It was almost as if he knew that Jazlyn was feeling anxious and worried about the big moment tomorrow.
She didn't want to let anybody down.

She said good night to her mom, dad and brother Jordie but couldn't go to sleep. She couldn't get her brain to stop thinking about tomorrow.

What if she fell walking up to the stage?

What if she forgot all of the words to the song?

What if the music doesn't play?

What if Mrs. Beggs were sick and not able to make it?

What if her voice cracked and she did a terrible job?

What if nobody liked her singing?

Every time Jazlyn thought of something that could go wrong, she could feel herself start to sweat. Her tummy started to hurt and she started thinking that maybe, she shouldn't do it.

“Jazlyn?” Mrs. J came back into the room. “I could hear you tossing and turning in here. Can’t you sleep?”

Jazlyn told her mom how she was worried about the singing tomorrow. She went over all of the ‘What ifs’ and waited for her mom to speak.

"Wow," Mrs. J looked at Jazlyn with wide eyes. "Those are a lot of NEGATIVE what ifs!" Jazlyn's mom nodded in agreement.

"But what about the WHAT IFS that you forgot?"

Jazlyn looked at her mom, surprised. There's MORE?, she thought.

"You said, 'What if you forgot the words to the song?' Well, WHAT IF your whole school sang along and helped you out?"

"What if the music doesn't play and you just keep going? Or what if someone stands by with backup music, ready to help you if there is something wrong with the original music?" Jazlyn's mom continued.

"What if the gym is filled with people waiting not just to hear you sing, but to honour Mrs. Beggs?"

“What if it is an incredibly special moment that Mrs. Beggs will never forget?”

“What if you finish and you hear the wonderful sound of applause and cheers?”

“Try not to focus on the negative ‘What ifs’ that rob you of enjoying the moment. Let yourself look ahead and see what a success you will be. You’ve prepared. You’ve practiced. Focus on the positive ‘What ifs’ that give you courage and happiness,” Jazlyn’s mom smiled.

“I was asked to give a speech once,” Jazlyn’s mom continued. “I was so nervous.” Jazlyn took her mother’s hand. She knew exactly how her mom felt.

“I spent so much time worrying about what could go wrong, I didn’t let myself think about what could go right!” Mrs. J chuckled to herself.

"I had this wonderful teacher who helped me get over my worry. The day before my speech, he said, 'You can do this. Tell me what is worrying you and we will plan ahead to make sure it doesn't happen.' "
Mrs. J smiled at the memory.

"So, we sat and made a list of the things I was worried about and we prepared a backup plan for all of them, including 'What if people laugh at me'?"

“What did he say?” Jazlyn asked anxiously. She really wanted to know.

“ ‘Take a breath and laugh along with them!’ my teacher had said. It was good advice. When I gave my speech, I actually forgot a line and stood in front of my whole school, looking out at my teacher for help. He smiled and gave me a thumbs up. I laughed and said, ‘So that just happened…’ Everyone laughed along with me. I think they knew how hard it can be to speak in front of people. He reminded me of my next line, and I went on and finished.”

Jazlyn giggled. That wasn’t so bad.

"So Jazlyn, if you make a mistake, take a deep breath and keep going. Whatever happens, you'll be ready. You have practiced, prepared and planned. You will do very well." Jazlyn smiled. She was ready. She could do this.

The next day, the gymnasium was filled with students, staff and parents. Everyone was there to honour Mrs. Beggs and wish her well as she leaves the school for a new adventure.

Jazlyn waited by the side of the stage in her favourite green dress and when she was introduced, the audience applauded politely. Jazlyn took a deep breath, walked out on stage and smiled at her wonderful teacher.

Mrs. Beggs smiled back and Jazlyn started to sing. Through the whole song, Mrs. Beggs would nod, smile warmly and put her hand to her heart. When the song was over, everyone clapped loudly and Mrs. Beggs jumped up from her seat to give Jazlyn a big hug.

It was a great moment. Jazlyn was so glad she had done it. She had indeed missed a word in the song but nobody seemed to notice and everyone, including Jazlyn's friends, thought she had done a fantastic job.

That night, Jazlyn and her family gathered to share their favourite parts of the day. This time Jazlyn couldn't wait to share her favourite parts. It had been such a great day.

"Hearing Jazlyn sing so beautifully today was my favourite part. I am so proud of you dear." Mr. J said.

“Oh, me too,” Mrs. J smiled. “You did a fantastic job! Mrs. Beggs seemed to love it.”

Her brother Jordie hugged her tight. Jazlyn figured he must have liked the song too.

“My favourite part of today was seeing how happy Mrs. Beggs was. And I am so glad I didn’t let the ‘What Ifs’ wreck that. I hope she has a great retirement and will always remember how much she means to all of us,” Jazlyn grinned, pleased at how well things had gone.

As she snuggled into bed, Jazlyn told herself that she will not let the negative thoughts get to her again. She would plan, prepare and practice for any speech, presentation or performance she may have to give in the future and let it all come together. She would always be ready for the 'What ifs'.